LARA CROFT:
Tomb Raider Hero

701-444-3785
librarian@co.mckenzie.nd.us

⭐ x1996

Kenny Abdo

Fly!
An Imprint of Abdo Zoom
abdobooks.com

abdobooks.com

Published by Abdo Zoom, a division of ABDO, P.O. Box 398166, Minneapolis,
Minnesota 55439. Copyright © 2021 by Abdo Consulting Group, Inc. International
copyrights reserved in all countries. No part of this book may be reproduced in any
form without written permission from the publisher. Fly!™ is a trademark and logo
of Abdo Zoom.

Printed in the United States of America, North Mankato, Minnesota.
052020
092020

**THIS BOOK CONTAINS
RECYCLED MATERIALS**

Photo Credits: Alamy, AP Images, Everette Collection, Flickr, Getty Images,
Shutterstock, ©BagoGames CC BY-SA 2.0 p.cover, 8, 15 / CC BY 2.0, ©Stefans02 p.4 /
CC BY 2.0, ©Glen Bowman p.16 / CC BY-SA 2.0
Production Contributors: Kenny Abdo, Jennie Forsberg, Grace Hansen
Design Contributors: Dorothy Toth, Neil Klinepier

Library of Congress Control Number: 2019956164

Publisher's Cataloging-in-Publication Data

Names: Abdo, Kenny, author.
Title: Lara Croft: Tomb Raider hero / by Kenny Abdo
Other title: Tomb Raider hero
Description: Minneapolis, Minnesota : Abdo Zoom, 2021 | Series: Video game heroes |
    Includes online resources and index.
Identifiers: ISBN 9781098221447 (lib. bdg.) | ISBN 9781644944189 (pbk.) |
    ISBN 9781098222420 (ebook) | ISBN 9781098222918 (Read-to-Me ebook)
Subjects: LCSH: Video game characters--Juvenile literature. | Croft, Lara (Fictitious
    character)--Juvenile literature. | Tomb raider (Video game : 2013)--Juvenile
    literature. | Sega Saturn video games--Juvenile literature. | Heroes--Juvenile
    literature.
Classification: DDC 794.8--dc23

TABLE OF CONTENTS

LARA CROFT

Raiding ancient tombs around the world, Lara Croft is the go-to guide for any adventure seeker!

With many video games, comic books, and movies, Croft has taken the *Tomb Raider* **franchise** to great places!

PLAYER PROFILE

Lara Croft and the Tomb Raider world was brought to life by a team of just six people. It usually takes a staff of hundreds to create a video game as complicated as *Tomb Raider*.

Creator Toby Gard envisioned the character as a man. To avoid comparisons with Indiana Jones, he changed the gender.

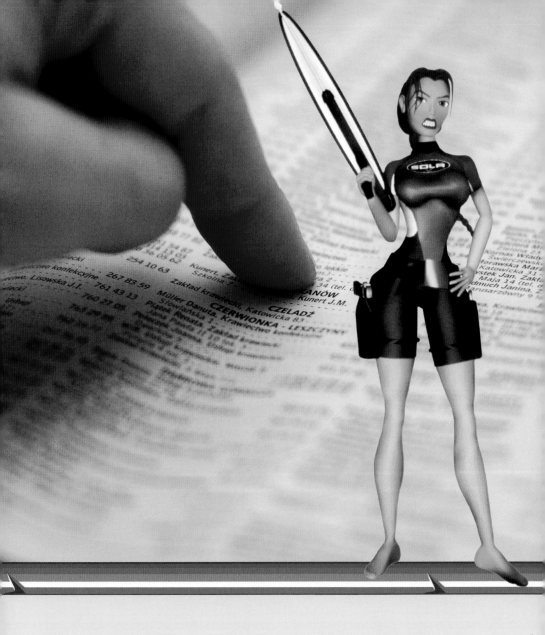

The crew knew that they wanted the character to be named Lara. They looked through the phone book to find the right last name. They liked one so much that they gave it to their hero, Lara Croft.

LEVEL UP

Croft dove into action with *Tomb Raider* in 1996. It was an unexpected success! It reached the top of sales charts selling more than 7 million copies.

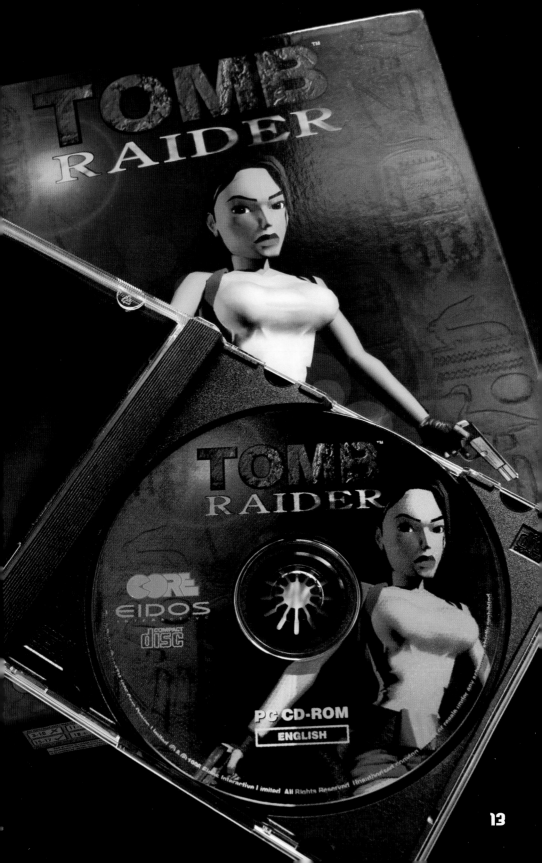

Tomb Raider II was also a success. Croft battled foes throughout China and Tibet for the Dagger of Xian.

Tomb Raider III saw Croft fighting through Antarctica. Later, *Tomb Raider: The Last Revelation* and *Chronicles* were created as **prequels**.

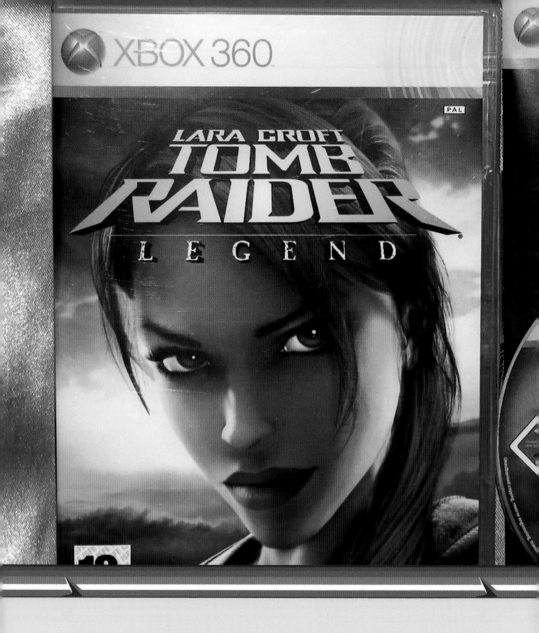

Tomb Raider: Legend came out in 2006. It was the first time the series was **rebooted**. Croft's **origin** was changed from previous games. In *Legend*, she searches for the famous **Excalibur**.

The *Tomb Raider* **franchise** was **rebooted** once again in 2013. Two additional adventures, *Rise of the Tomb Raider* and *Shadow of Tomb Raider* were released.

RISE OF THE
TOMB RAIDER™

EXPANSION PACK

Croft is one of the most popular **cosplay** costumes. She has also appeared on more than 1,200 magazine covers. Not even the most famous superstars have done that!

In 2001 and 2003, Academy Award winner Angelina Jolie portrayed Croft on the big screen. Alicia Vikander took the torch and stepped into Croft's boots for the 2018 adventure.

Croft made the *Guinness Book of World Records*. She is the best-selling video game heroine, proving Croft is who you want on your side on a dangerous adventure!

ES JUNE 15

MOVIE.COM

GLOSSARY

cosplay – short for costume play. To dress up as a character from a cartoon, movie, or video game.

Excalibur – the legendary sword of King Arthur.

franchise – a series of related works each of which includes the same characters that interact in the same fictional universe.

origin – the point where something begins.

prequel – a story that takes place before the story of an existing work.

reboot – a new start to a video game franchise, recreating plots, characters, and backstory.

ONLINE RESOURCES

Booklinks
NONFICTION NETWORK
FREE! ONLINE NONFICTION RESOURCES

To learn more about
Lara Croft, please visit
abdobooklinks.com or scan
this QR code. These links
are routinely monitored
and updated to provide the
most current information
available.

INDEX